SPACE CAT EXPLORES STEM

The World Humans Made

by Jacqueline A. Ball
illustrations by Ken Bowser

RED CHAIR
•PRESS•

Please visit our website at **www.redchairpress.com** for more
high-quality products for young readers.

About the Author

Jacqueline A. Ball is a Seattle-based writer, editor, and the
former publisher of Scientific American Books for Kids and Weekly
Reader Juvenile Book Clubs. Awards and honors include Booklist
Top 10 Youth Series Nonfiction (ALA), Children's Choice and Parents'
Choice Honors.

Publisher's Cataloging-In-Publication Data
Names: Ball, Jacqueline A. | Bowser, Ken, illustrator.
Title: The world humans made / by Jacqueline A. Ball ; illustrations by Ken Bowser.

Description: South Egremont, MA : Red Chair Press, [2017] | Series: Space Cat explores STEM
    | Interest age level: 006-009. | Aligned to: Next Generation SCIENCE Standards. | Includes
    glossary, Did You Know sidebars and Try It! feature. | Includes bibliographical references
    and index. | Summary: "People use creative or inventive thinking to adapt the natural
    world to help them meet their needs or wants. All people use tools and technology in
    their life and jobs to solve problems. Join Space Cat and her friend Dog as they compare
    the natural world and the world humans made. Discover how STEM skills play a role."--
    Provided by publisher.

Identifiers: LCCN 2016954284 | ISBN 978-1-63440-194-4 (library hardcover) |
    ISBN 978-1-63440-198-2 (paperback) | ISBN 978-1-63440-202-6 (ebook)

Subjects: LCSH: Technology--Juvenile literature. | Inventions--Juvenile literature. |
    CYAC: Technology. | Inventions.

Classification: LCC T47 .B35 2017 (print) | LCC T47 (ebook) | DDC 600--dc23

Photo Credits: Shutterstock, Inc.

Space Cat Explores STEM first published by:
Red Chair Press LLC   PO Box 333   South Egremont, MA 01258-0333

Printed in the United States of America
0517 1P CGBF17

Look around you. What do you see?

If you are in school, you might see desks, books, and **computers**. If you are outdoors, you might see trees and cars and buildings. You see all these things at the same time, but here is a surprise. They come from two different worlds.

One world is the world of nature. The other world is the world humans made. Humans created the things in it to make living in the world of nature easier, safer, and more fun. They used their imaginations. They also used science and math.

Join Space Cat and her friend Dog as they explore the world humans made.

Look for important new words in **bold** letters.

Can you name 5 things in this picture that are part of the world of nature?

Every living thing is part of the world of nature, from the tiniest ant to the tallest tree. Rocks and rivers, rain and snow, and the moon and stars are all part of the **natural world** too.

Did You Know?

Space Cat:
Humans are part of the natural world. So are cats.

Dog:
Don't forget dogs!

5

Buildings and bridges are part of the world humans made. Airplanes and light bulbs and computers are part of that world too. Pencils, scissors, toothbrushes, and other **tools** are all part of the **human-made world**.

It takes a lot of skills to design and build bridges!

Think about the skills needed to design an airplane that can stay in the sky.

Did You Know?

Dog:
Humans who plan and make buildings and bridges are called **engineers**.

Space Cat:
Engineers plan and build all kinds of **machines** to use on Earth and in space. Rockets are my favorite!

The two worlds exist together,
but they are different.

Try it!

Look at the pictures. On a piece of paper, write down all the things that are part of the natural world. On another piece of paper, write down all the things that are part of the human-made world.

Work with a friend or make teams! Try to think of five more things from each world, human-made and natural. You will come up with the best ideas and have the most fun when you **collaborate**.

The very first humans did not live in
two worlds. They lived only in the
natural world. It was not easy! There
were big problems.
Wild animals wanted to
eat them. Snow and rain
made them cold and wet.

11

Early humans looked around the natural world for **solutions**. They found caves to live in. Then they figured out how to use animal skins and bones to build huts. Years later, they built stronger huts out of mud, twigs, and bricks. They were the first engineers!

Places to stay safe from bad weather and danger are called **shelters**. All creatures need shelter to survive.

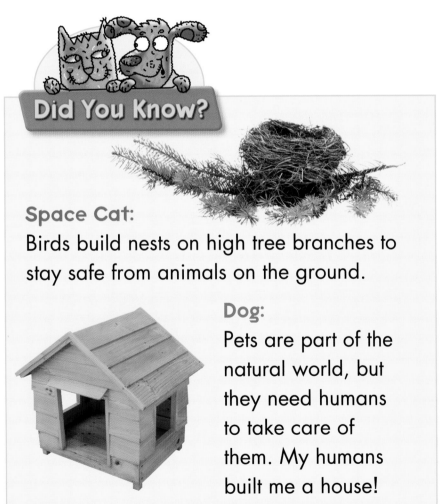

Did You Know?

Space Cat:
Birds build nests on high tree branches to stay safe from animals on the ground.

Dog:
Pets are part of the natural world, but they need humans to take care of them. My humans built me a house!

Humans use STEM skills to keep our homes warm and safe.

Humans wanted to make their shelters better. They built places for fire to keep them warm. The light from the fire helped scare away wild animals. For thousands of years, humans have kept inventing new ways to make their shelters safer and more comfortable.

Today **electricity** lights our homes and makes washing machines and refrigerators work. Heating **systems** built by engineers keep our homes warm.

Did You Know?

Space Cat:
Humans did not invent fire. Fire is part of the natural world. It was a **discovery** that may have happened when lightning hit a tree and set it on fire.

Humans wanted to make their work easier, too. Thousands of years ago, the only way to move something heavy was to drag it along the ground. That took a long time and made everyone very tired. Then someone thought of cutting a slice from a tree trunk to make a wheel. People made wagons to roll heavy things. Sometimes animals pulled the wagons. It made work for humans much easier!

Did You Know?

Space Cat:
The first wheels were solid. Later on, humans made wheels with **spokes**. They were lighter and faster.

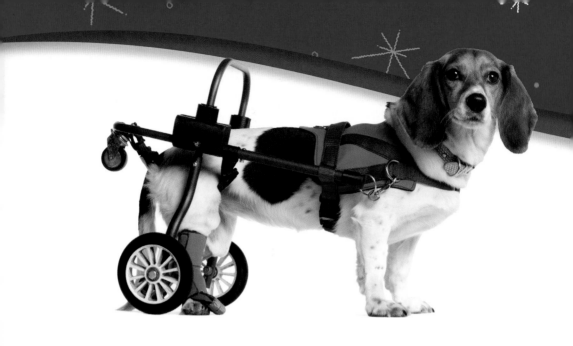

Today wheels are everywhere.

Can you imagine a world without them?

Here are some things humans made after they invented the wheel. Can you think of some others? Write them down on a piece of paper. Draw one thing with wheels you use every day.

19

Another name for the tools and machines humans invented to solve problems and make life better is **technology**. Technology is always changing, because scientists and engineers are always thinking up new ways to make human lives easier, safer, and more fun.

Today we have computers, the **Internet**, and smartphones. What do you think will come next?

Engineers follow steps called the **design process** as they come up with solutions. One part of the process is to draw a **sketch** of their idea. Then they keep improving it. What would you invent to make your life or someone else's life better? Find a large sheet of paper and make a sketch. Use a pencil with an eraser so you can keep improving your idea. Collaborate with friends or teammates. Maybe your **invention** will change the world!

Glossary

Collaborate Work with another person or a team

Computer A machine that stores and works with information

Design process Series of steps engineers take as they plan a solution to a problem

Discovery Something in the natural world that is seen or understood for the first time

Electricity A kind of energy that travels on wires

Engineers Humans who plan and make equipment, machines, and buildings

Human-made world Every thing humans built or created

Internet A giant network that connects computers all over the world

Invention Something made by a human that makes life better and did not exist before, such as the light bulb

Machine A piece of equipment with moving parts that needs power to work

Natural world Plants, animals, oceans, planets, and everything else not made by humans

Shelter A building that protects living things from danger and bad weather

Sketch A simple drawing

Solutions Ways to solve problems

Spokes Bars going from the center of a wheel to the rim

System A group of parts that work together

Technology Scientific inventions and new ideas that solve problems and make life better for people

Tool An object made by humans to do a certain job

Learn More in the Library

Books

Podesto, Martine. *My Science Notebook: Inventions.* Gareth Stevens Publishing, 2009

Turner, Tracey; Mills, Andrea; Gifford, Clive. *100 Inventions That Made History*. DK Publishing, 2014

Woodcock, Jon. *Coding Games in Scratch.* DK Kids, 2015

Web Sites

NASA Kids Club
nasa.gov/audience/forstudents/k-4/index.html

PBS Kids Design Squad
pbskids.org/designsquad/

index